Garden design and landscaping 2020

A SIMPLE STEP BY STEP GUIDE ABOUT HOME LANDSCAPE DESIGN FOR BEGINNERS TO CREATE PLANT COMBINATIONS FOR AN ABUNDANT GARDEN

TABLE OF CONTENTS

Introduction

When I talk about landscaping, I'm thinking about something between these two extremes. Yes, you should dream a bit when planning your home garden, but of course your plans must be rooted in reality. The landscape is actually all of the above. It's the total outdoor environment. The landscape might refer to large parks and open spaces or smaller urban areas. As individuals we don't have much control over design of the larger landscape. However, we have total control over our "yard" or the immediate environment around our home. Why not make the most of it? Make it more appealing, more enjoyable. Make it special!

Actually, I prefer the term "home garden" to "yard" or "landscape". My idea of a garden is not just a vegetable bed. When speaking of the home garden I picture images of walkways, outdoor seating areas, open views or privacy screens, interesting small spaces with eye catching features such as statuary, a novelty plant or a water fountain. It's all that and more. It's the view from the street or the view from the kitchen window. With this in mind, landscaping is MUCH more than just decoration. We can make it whatever we want. Your outdoor living spaces should be a continuation of the home's interior and should not only match, but add to the style of the home.

Our typical American style of landscaping puts emphasis on the appearance of the house from the street. The "public area", the perspective from the street, is typically designed to decorate the home creating "curb appeal". However, in many other countries around the world, there would be a wall near the street with the plantings inside the wall creating a garden view from inside the house. Think about it. Your home IS your castle. It's your biggest asset. It is your refuge from the "jungle". It's where you relax, recuperate and entertain friends. It's where you live! Make the most of it. Make your home environment welcoming to visitors. Make it comfortable, pleasant and interesting. Make it exciting!

Ok now that we're starting to see the big

picture, how about this "rooted in reality" idea? A well designed landscape should do more than just decorate your house. Properly placed trees will cool or warm your house as needed. Well-designed beds will make mowing and maintenance much simpler. Walkways should facilitate movement around your house and welcome guests. Are you starting to get the picture? So many landscape features can either be an asset or a liability. It's all a matter of what you plant and where. I think you'd agree it's important enough to deserve a well thought out plan.

As mentioned above, the well- designed garden space should provide beauty, privacy, relaxation, entertainment and enjoyment for many years to come. It's not a short term proposition. Garden development takes years. We're dealing with trees here. Unfortunately, in our mobile American society many people think in the near term. We often plan on moving in a few short years for various reasons. But, even in this case, proper landscaping will provide a few years of enjoyment and a return on investment when you sell. But the big rewards come after many years of growth and development of a properly planned, installed and maintained garden. More than just increasing your property value, "the right plant in the right place" can truly result in an increase in your enjoyment and quality of life!

Sadly when driving down just about any residential street in America I see many cases of plantings done with little or no forethought. Often potentially large trees are positioned where they will crowd the house, walks or driveway. I see shrubs sheared into boxes and balls to keep them in bounds. But I also see shrubs growing up into the windows or plants that are colorful for only a short time in summer located in the public area where they are seen year around, even when they are dormant and not very attractive (more on this later). Or maybe it's combinations of plants with no thought to their flower colors, flowering sequence or the general appearance in all seasons of the year. With better knowledge of plant material and a well thought out design, this picture could be pleasant in every season with far less maintenance. One secret to low maintenance is to strive for a natural appearance. A natural look can be a little "loose on the edges" and not so structured or "man-made". With the right plant in the right place heavy shearing isn't necessary. The chosen plants should fill in their allotted space, choking out many weeds in the process.

Chapter - 1
THE FUNDAMENTAL OF LANDSCAPE DESIGN

As a landscape designer for over 20 years, I have run across a multitude of spaces needing attention, whether they had started as a blank slate or had become an area that was overgrown and neglected. The process of landscape design involves a series of steps that build upon one another, so I will start from the beginning with the basics. The more planning you do initially will lead to better results when your project is completed.

Function: When discussing function, consider the purpose you would like your landscape to achieve. If it is a quiet place you desire, then perhaps adding a small stone patio and or garden bench could create a peaceful retreat. If looking to attract wildlife, then the addition of a water feature, birdbath or feeder could also be part of the thought process. Of course, function may be on a wider scale, such as the desire for a patio or deck, pool, or outdoor grilling and entertaining space. Once function is determined, other factors are then considered in the process of landscape design.

Unity and Balance: When designing, the different landscape elements should look like they belong together. Areas can be tied into one another by repeating some elements such as form, color, and texture throughout the landscape. The use of similar groupings of plantings can help to achieve this effect. It is also helpful to limit the number of different types of plants you are using so that the design doesn't become too "busy." Groupings of certain plants in odd numbers, such as groups of three, five, or seven create a sense of flow and simple repetition, giving a stronger sense of unity. Odd numbers also allow for variations in height and are often perceived as a single unit that is not easily visually divided.

Balance can be achieved through symmetry. Symmetrical balance is achieved when the same objects (mirror images) are placed on either side of an axis, while the asymmetrical balance is achieved by equal visual weight of non-equal amounts of form, color, or texture on either side of an axis. For example, while designing a front foundation planting, a grouping of flowering

Spirea 'Magic Carpet' can be used on one side of a stoop, while a grouping of burgundy colored 'Spilled Wine' Weigela can be used on the opposite side. In this case the balance is asymmetrical with different foliage types and flowering times. In another example, a Hinoki Cypress with a grouping of daylilies repeated on each side of a front stoop would create an exact mirror image of symmetrical balance. The use of either symmetrical or asymmetrical balance will create the same effect of unity and flow in the landscape.

Form: The shape of an object as defined by a line is referred to as form in garden design. Form is probably one of the most important elements in designing a landscape. It is what is seen when first looking at a garden from a distance. Every plant has a distinct growth-habit and shape which develops and changes over time as the plant matures. These shapes, whether upright, weeping, columnar, pyramidal, spreading, or round, define the spaces in the garden.

When describing the line of the bed, generally, straight lines depict a more formal setting, while curvilinear lines create a more informal look. It is best to run the same theme throughout the space to encourage uniformity. Also, be sure that the scaling, or size relationship between elements within a setting and its surrounding areas is appropriate. Taller trees can be used to soften and bring down the scale of a building, while smaller shrubs can be used along a foundation, such as under a window. When deciding on the type of bed outline or line of plant placement, I first look at the architecture of the home and any existing hardscape that is going to stay intact. If there are mostly straight lines, the design can be one of a more conservative style using straight beds with slight curves or placement of plants could be straight-lined rather than staggered. The opposite holds if they are many curves in the architecture of the building or any other factors of the hardscape. The use of curvilinear, or curved lines would then create more of an informal garden. The two styles can be combined if done carefully, but it is generally better to stick to one theme.

Color: Color plays an important role in garden design and is often more difficult to achieve in winter. It is best to plant perennials that complement one another (warm and cool hues) and those that have varying bloom times. For example, the deep purple blooms of 'May Night' Salvia (cool hue) are striking against the bright yellow blooms of Daylily 'Stella D Oro' (warm hue). The bluish-lavender blooms of Nepeta 'Walkers Low' (cool hue) complement the delicate yellow blooms of Coreopsis 'Zagreb' (warm hue). For all year color, add colorful evergreen shrubs such as Blue Globe Spruce, Gold Mop Cypress, Gold Lace Juniper, or Blue Star Juniper. For seasonal interest, add flowering shrubs that bloom at different intervals, such as spirea, weigela, azalea, rhododendron, forthysia, buddleia (butterfly bush), or syringa (lilac), to name a few. Take into consideration the fact that foliage and bloom colors of perennials and shrubs do change with each season. The idea is to disperse color equally among the four seasons to keep the garden constantly looking at its best. It is also important to have a sense of unity and repetition to make the design "flow." Be sure to mass similar plantings for maximum color, and as mentioned, combine colorful evergreens, deciduous shrubs, and perennials for all-season interest. It is also important to reuse the same plantings throughout the garden for maximum consistency.

Texture: There are three types of plant texture: fine, medium, and coarse. Plants with fine foliage are those with small, feathery, or narrow leaves, such as various types of ferns, sedges, grasses or some varieties of Japanese maple. Plants exhibiting coarse texture display large, voluminous leaves, such as those' of hosta or elephant ears. Ranging in between are those plants with medium texture. Some plants that come to mind for exhibiting good texture, which I have incorporated into many of my designs, include Japanese Forest Grass (Hakonechloa macra), hosta, Japanese Painted Fern, golden oriental sedge, ornamental grasses, Heuchera (Coral Bells), liriope, leucothoe, Weeping Japanese Maple, dwarf white pine, dwarf globe blue spruce, and weeping Norway spruce, just to mention a few.

Environmental Conditions-What to Plant Where: When selecting plants, there are several environmental factors to consider, such as the lighting and soil requirements, cold hardiness, size of a mature plant, and insect resistance.

There are three main lighting requirements for plants, those that grow best in shade, those that require full sun, and those that need somewhere in between.

When discussing soil types, there are numerous scenarios. Clay soils, which appear as orange-tinged in hue, tend to retain much moisture and do not drain freely. Sandy soils, usually light in color and sometimes rocky are the opposite, allowing moisture to pass right through, while loamy soils are rich in organic matter and hold water in moderation. Many plants do not fare well sitting in water retained by a heavy clay soil, while others thrive in wet conditions. Some plants prefer a well-drained soil, or one containing a significant percentage of sand, where water will not accumulate. The best combination is a mixture of all three soil types. Along with soil composition, pH is also important, as many plants prefer a slightly acidic soil (such as rhododendron and azalea) verses plants that may thrive best in a more neutral, or even basic soil. Overall, it is important to carefully note the preferred soil conditions for your plants before planting and plan accordingly for the best success.

When it comes to cold hardiness, specific zone maps have been developed to categorize climates based on the lowest minimum temperature and highest maximum temperature. Always try to choose plants that fall somewhere in the middle of the range for your zone. For example, if your location is in zone 7, plant varieties that are hardy in zones 4-8 should be used to ensure survival. If your area happens to get a severely cold winter with sustained temperatures near the zero-degree mark, it could mimic a much colder climate, causing plants to go into distress. The opposite is true with hotter than normal conditions. If the plant you purchase is hardy in zones 4-8, there will be a much better chance of your plant thriving should your area experience any adverse conditions. Choosing plants that are hardy in zones slightly warmer and cooler than the one you are in will alleviate any issues with survival.

There are several factors to take into consideration when planning your space. Following these basic design principles along with the information to follow will assist you in creating a welcoming and functional outdoor environment.

Chapter - 2
KNOWING EVERYTHING BEFORE TO START

A lot of people have dreams of having the most amazing front or back yard, the entertaining space to dazzle their friends and be the life of the town and the place to be for social get-togethers but have absolutely no idea of where to begin. Most start with small-scale DIY projects such as flowers around the front porch, maybe a little mulch around the trees, or even a small raised garden with a few herbs (The legal kind, bring it back to reality little dreamer). That is certainly sensible, but time-consuming. It could take years to get to the place that you have envisioned.

Some get somewhat of a design together based on what they see around them. These days, it's all about "Keeping up with the Jones'". Everyone trying to have the latest and greatest to get the neighbors talking and get the adulation they so vehemently desire so they immediately go into massive debt to get there. Whatever the case may be, landscapers and other contractors are raking it in.

Still, others are more methodical and get a game plan, save for each piece of the puzzle and for a few years, end up with the "Dream" entertaining space. This is usually the best option for everyone involved. Over the years, I've seen a ton of different scenarios from a full-blown paradise, to what I can only describe as a "Used car graveyard", to a hodgepodge of odds and ends scattered around the yard.

Whatever the case may be, whichever situation you are in or what category you may fall into, like any truly great story, start at the beginning and work your way to the final destination. Take the journey step by step, plan every little detail, and finally, DO YOUR RESEARCH! I cannot stress this enough. Whenever I go out to do an estimate, I always ask if they have had any other contractors scheduled as well. Sometimes, I end up losing a project because I'm not always the "Cheapest" option and I tell everyone that upfront. BUT, I AM the best option, because I will listen to the customer, get a thorough idea of what they want, and, if I don't feel I'm the best fit for them, I will tell them. I believe in being honest and real with customers, it's all about them, not me.

The best place to start is to draw a map. Not a typical map but more of a timeline. Take a good long look at where your yard/entertaining space is now and put it at the beginning. Look at catalogs, the internet, local home improvement stores, etc. and find the elements you would like to have and add those. Make sure you're doing this on paper, whiteboard, etc. so you can SEE the path. Believe it or not, this will help you make the best decisions and come to the ultimate conclusion.

Like any other major purchase, you need to have a game plan. You certainly wouldn't buy a house or a car sight-unseen would you? I didn't think so. Therefore, you need to develop your timeline to make things smooth. Take pictures of elements you like, things you see while your out and about, or save pictures you see online. Don't make impulse buys or fall for some "Snake oil salesman" when it comes to improving your home. Your home is your castle, treat it as such.

Once you have a game plan together, and this is THE most important part, STICK TO IT!!! Do not get hit by "Shiny object syndrome". Just because something may look awesome at the moment, it may not be right for what you're trying to accomplish. Take a picture, think about it overnight. Trust me, it will be there tomorrow. Once you find a decent, respectable landscape/hardscape contractor, which you will learn about in Chapter 5, they will listen to you, ask questions, and be able to show you a 3D rendering that should reflect everything you are trying to put together.

Locating Resources

There are several ways to locate the resources you need to have the space of your dreams. You have Google, phone book, referrals, and several websites that will contractors contact you after you fill out the form stating what you're looking for. Don't go with the first one that contacts you. Get at least 3 estimates for whatever the project is and weigh the options. Using the home and car example from above, you wouldn't buy a car from the first lot you go to, would you? I didn't think so.

Any home addition must be considered a major purchase as it affects your home's value. Think of the proverbial "Pebble in the Pond" effect. Before-tax assessment season, you decide to add a fire pit and benches in the back yard. The tax assessor notices this and your property taxes go up to $300/year. It doesn't sound like much but unless you're rolling in cash, it can be a major hit.

Now that you have compiled a list of contractors, take a couple of days and research each one.

Look at both positive and negative reviews. Look them up on BBB.org and see what kind of rating they have if they have any unresolved complaints. If everything checks out, compare them all, and choose the best one. Remember, "You get what you pay for". I have to explain this a lot to potential customers when I go out to do estimates. I tell them all, "Yes, you can go with the cheaper option, and when that fails in 3-5 years, I'll be here."

Once you have the contractors, contact them. Explain your plans, and have them come out to give you an estimate. This will give you a solid projection of how much it's going to take to get your project done. Then you are one step closer to realizing your dream space.

As I said before, get at least 3 estimates for each project and compare them all. I cannot stress this enough. You never want to put all your eggs into one basket, ever! Now that you have your estimates, spend some time looking at the details. See what each one is going to include and if any of them aren't exactly what you're looking for, contact them and ask them to amend the estimate to show exactly what you're asking for. Look at the timeline each one gives. How long is it going to take to complete the project? Do they show a breakdown of every element? Look at the charge for labor, this will tell you a lot about the contractor as well. For example, if two of them show a labor cost of $3,000 and the third shows $900, RED FLAG!!! More than likely, that contractor utilizes undocumented help or they don't know what they're doing. Don't get me wrong, I have nothing against someone trying to make a living, but in my 13 plus years of construction experience, those situations never end well.

Something else to look at is "Equipment". The same rule applies, if one is completely different from the others, think about it first. Most, if not all, equipment rental companies charge about the same for their equipment. Even if the contractor has their equipment, they're still going to charge the same as if they were renting it. This helps them cover fuel, repairs, and normal wear and tear on the equipment.

One final note on looking at your estimates: Read the fine print at the bottom. I have several items in my contracts to cover my rear end when it comes to customers. These days, everyone wants something for nothing so most, if not all contractors put in fine print different penalties for cancellations, changes, etc. If you have any questions, ASK. As I've been told many, many times, don't be afraid to ask. Remember, it's your money going out the door. Once all these steps are completed, you are then ready to move on to the next one.

Setting Your Budget

Setting your budget is one of the most important steps. However you decide to pay for this new venture, whether it be with credit cards, cash, or financing, you need to have a reasonable budget set aside for it. If I had a nickel for every time I asked a potential customer what they're budget was like so that I could work within that and still get them what they're looking for, I wouldn't have to work for a living. Make sure that you do your research when setting a budget. Do not expect Tiffany products at Wal-Mart prices. Remember, you get what you pay for so if your budget cheap, you're going to get cheap. There's a quote that I use a lot when talking to potential customers, "Good work is not cheap, and cheap work is not good". Let that sink in for a minute, I'll wait.

Figure out how much you want to add, where you want to add it and go from there. If you know you can only afford to add a retaining wall, for now, then budget as such. If you prefer to have the patio first, then plan accordingly. Never get in over your head. You don't want to go into massive debt to get the whole package now when you can prioritize, set the proper budget, and get what you want in

s. I've had customers start with a patio, come back a few months later, get a fire pit, benches, and retaining wall, then a few months after that, a gorgeous water feature. Now, they're the envy of the neighborhood. All because they budgeted correctly, paid for it all with cash they saved up, and had a realistic plan.

When deciding on a budget, there are many factors but, again, you have to prioritize. Consider everything you want to have done, write it down and go over the list. What do you have to have done first? What can wait until you save up some more? See where this is going? Put your list on paper, see it, visualize it, and go from there. It gives you a more tangible element to look at. When you can see your goals on paper, your thought process becomes a lot clearer than just going over it in your head.

Chapter - 3
LAND SCAPE DESIGN GUIDELINES

First, design your landscape on paper. Begin by listing the functions your landscape should provide your family, such as play areas for small children, entertainment areas, and shade. Next, decide where these functional areas should be located for maximum pleasure and use. Consider wind patterns, sunlight, accessibility, and other site-specific conditions when creating your landscape plan.

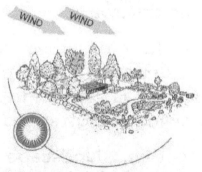

Here are some useful facts to consider when designing your landscape:

- when selecting plants, consider function first and foremost. Next, decide on acceptable maintenance levels. Group plants according to irrigation needs whenever possible.

- always select plants according to how their mature size and appearance fit into your design. Do not select plants based on initial appearance in immature stage of growth.

- Consider adding interest and color to your landscape by rotating annual flowers in small "investment zones" near your house.

- Plants that are placed by themselves and directly exposed to the sky are more frost prone than those protected by shade from other plants, patios, or other structures.

- large growing trees should be planted at least 20 feet from your house. This gives tree roots adequate space to grow and prevents structural damage to your home. Also avoid planting trees closer than five feet from sidewalks and driveways.

Paths in a carefully designed sequence, or applied on a larger scale to the movement of people in cars, such as the design of motorway planting for viewing at high speeds.

Unlike architecture, landscape design is concerned with living material, which not only grows changes during the season & over time, but also moves in response to wind or to the touch. Thus the kinetic experience is enriched and made more intimate and varied. The positioning of groups of planting relatives to the path can influence the movement of the observer.

Where a change of direction is desired, ground covers as well as tree & accent shrubs can be used to create pivots point at which one is physically and visually forced to change direction. Pivot points can be extended to form bridging points across paths & roads. If the bridging points are sited close together, these in turn create tension points in the design where the space is narrowed down or constricted before opening up & expanding into another space. Using the idea of line of line of movement, the design can be given a momentum of its own which can be described as a "design speed'. This can be static, slow, and moderate or fast; the inherent design force built into any line movement is self-expressive.

Certain misconception exists relating to design line movement. All too often designers seek to create line movement by giving a wavy outline to planting beds. Tree & shrub planting will itself create all the wavy line movement at a higher level as it grows.

Plant material junction should not be too acute.

Where the design line movement abuts a building, or two paved areas meets grass areas, the acute point formed results in an awkward space for planting & should be avoided where possible.

Access, Vistas and Arrangement: The point of entry into any given space is always of crucial importance in the design. For instance, one may choose to make it discreet or emphasize it by enfacement. A drive or access road into a site may have predominantly vista -like qualities, which can be reinforced with banks of tall & medium shrub & ground cover. Planting flanking each side. The long accepted tradition that when one entered a site, part of the building was first seen & then lost from view, to reemerge later, still remains an effective design technique.

The principle of enfacement can be used effectively to draw attention to specifically desirable views & possibly to block out the less desirable elements. For instance massed foreground planting may be used to screen the near view, larger framing plants placing the emphasis on the distant view. Enfacement of certain views in connection with doorways or atrium courtyards can best be achieved by the use of large vertical shrubs or small trees with a horizontal branches structure.

Anchoring as a design technique is akin to enfacement in so far as it has a similar design purpose that is to control corners & portion of the design which need reinforcement. The planting of dome-shaped shrubs at the base of small sculptural tree or shrub is another form of anchoring.

Landscape Design Guidelines

- The walls, ceiling and floor are the dimensions of the outdoor "room". A ceiling (the sky) and a floor (the ground) are always present, though they might require modifications. The walls are created as part of the landscape design.

- The structure of anyone of the three dimensions mentioned above may affect the appearance of the other two as well as their functions.

- The landscape's walls are responsible for screening, wind protection, framing of off property views, enclosure, and so forth.

- The ceiling of the landscape provide shade, protection from weather elements, passive solar heating, and so forth.

- Structural walls for the landscape include many types of walls and fences. They offer the advantages of full height from the start, limited ground-coverage, and variety of materials.

- The most satisfactory landscape walls often combine both structural and planting materials.

- The principle concerned with ceiling structure in the landscape is for shading purpose. Shade may be provided by structural roods, awning, arbors, or the like or by shade and ornamental trees.

- Good shading units depends on accurate recognition of the time of day when the shade is necessary, the path of the sun over a property, and the angle at which the sun penetrates the area during the time shade is needed. Further recognition of the density of shade desired is also necessary.

- Tree placement must be based, in part on above and below ground utility structures that might be affected by -or affect -the tree's branches or roots.

- The light and shadow patterns created by the landscape's ceiling structure are extremely importantly aesthetically.

- The characteristics of plants are form, texture and color.

- The giant forms in native vegetation tend to conform to the natural landforms of that area.

- Trees may be used to obstruct awkward angles and lines in the building without distorting other landscaping features.

- Berms can successfully make a flat building lot seem more a part of the larger, rolling countryside, effectively making a property seem larger.

- Textural coordination between plant materials, building materials, and other non-living landscape elements result in better composition.

- Complementarycolorsinsubtlecombinations are usually better than stark contrasts that command too much attention.

- The more elaborate the trim elements in the building or other structural parts of the landscape, the simpler the design should be, with less contrast in color, texture and form and vice versa. Plant selection should always be based on specifications built during the design process and without consideration of personal prejudices.

- Plant selection should begin with only those plants climatically adapted to the area in which they are to be planted.

- The moisture retention capabilities, pH, and

fertility of a soil determine its capacity for growing healthy plants.

- Soil contains minerals, water, humus, living organisms, and air; it is the combination of these elements that determines the soil's suitability for plant growth.

- Optimum sun and shade combinations should always be known for plants so that they can be combined with site features, preventing sun related plant injuries and bringing out the best in plant growth, form and color.

- That colors change with seasons, alteration interview distance, and amount of light available must be given thought as plants are chosen for color contributions to the landscape.

- When it is possible to spread a sequence of blooms throughout the season, color clashes are avoided and blooms have a longer lasting effect on the landscape.

- The specific use being made of a plant and the landscape must be considered during its selection. In many cases, the special uses dictate the varieties.

- Texture of plant range from fine through course. The stems, leaves, bark create texture and buds and can be seen and felt.

- Simplicity, variety, emphasis, balance sequence, and scale are all applied to the composition of a unified landscape planting.

- Whenever variable elements are used in a planting unit, emphasis is created. The designer's job is to place greater emphasis where it is warranted.

- Good balance may be either symmetrical or asymmetrical. Balance must exist not only from side to side also from foreground to background of view.

- As planting units are designed, all possible viewing angles should be considered. The principles of composition must apply for typical viewing points as well as when moving through the landscape.

- A point of emphasis in a planting unit is often called a focal point. It may be created by means of an accent plant, a specimen plant serving as accent plant, a hard element, or landscape embellishment.

- To control a landscape design, each unit must be designed within itself, since the viewer is incapable of viewing the whole, but units must also relate favorably to one another to tie the landscape together.

- Trying design ideas simultaneously in elevation view and plant view is a good way for the designer to form accurate mental images. Plants should be represented at mature size.

- Individual plants may have qualities that make them suitable for accenting, massing or as specimen plants standing alone.

- Designing in elevation and plan simultaneously without considering individual plant varieties result in the building of a set of plant specifications without prejudice for favorite varieties.

- Though buildings can be designed to match their surroundings better, often the landscape designer must work with mismatched architecture.

- Elevation drawings are helpful, as the designer can use them to overlay building features with projected landscape concepts.

- A focal point may be created at an entryway by a sequence of color or texture or both. Embellishments may be used for accent, or ground pattern lines may direct attention appropriately.

Items for Backyard Landscaping

If you are fortunate enough to have a backyard, you already have the beginnings of what could soon be the most relaxing area of your home.

After a long week of work all of us desire a place to go where it is peaceful and restful. With the proper planning for backyard landscaping ideas your backyard could be this retreat. We will discuss several ideas for backyard landscaping.

Flowers, Trees, and other Plants

One of the best ways to create your own personal paradise is to create a garden of "Eden" in your backyard. You can do this by creating gardens, planting your favorite types of trees, especially fruit trees, and by planting other plants. When it comes to creating a spectacular garden there are many types of gardens to choose from, many of them are simple and inexpensive to create. A rock garden is one of the easiest gardens to create and all you need are plenty of rocks, plenty of your favorite flowers, a little time, and some imagination.

Water Features

Adding water features to your backyard is one of the best methods of backyard landscaping. There are many different water features on the market, or you can easily create your own water feature. Whether you purchase a water feature or create your own, they are simple and inexpensive to create. The best part is that a water feature can be worth its weight in gold when it comes to adding beauty to your backyard and making your backyard more enjoyable. There is nothing more relaxing than listening to the sound of running water.

Gazebos

Another way that many people make their backyard livable is to add a gazebo. Gazebos are inexpensive, and can be constructed by the homeowner in most cases. A gazebo adds a comfortable place to relax or have cookouts and other family gatherings. You can also decorate your gazebo with flowers, water features, and other decorations to add even more luxury to your backyard.

Chapter - 4
LOW-COST, EASY RAISED BEDS FOR YOUR LANDSCAPING

After selecting the plants for your garden, it's time to find a suitable place for them. Raised beds offer several benefits to creative landscapers who are looking for a low-cost and low maintenance garden.

Raised bed planting improves growing conditions for plants and provides interesting contours and depth to the landscape. You can create raised beds with a variety of objects. You can use slate, brick, landscape ties, wood timbers or any flat stone for retaining walls. Secure wooden ties with landscape tie nails and if built correctly, you don't have to use cement for stone walls.

A simple approach is creating berms to plant trees. Mound soil to create small, sweeping hills and plant trees on it. Berm creates height and interest in the landscape and if you feel retaining walls are not necessary then don't use them.

Don't make berms too high, instead of a sharp incline they should have a gradual slope. Berms with a sharpinclines erode at a faster pace. Make your berm only a few feet tall and five to seven times as long and width same length to its height. This simply means 1foot high berm should be 5 to 7 feet wide. This ratio will steady the berm, ensure soil, mulch and plants don't slide off after a rainstorm.

You can create a berm with just high-quality topsoil or you can use well-drained sandy loam underneath and only the top 1 foot of the berm containing high-quality topsoil. The volume of soil depends on what you are planting on the berm. If you are planting a shrub or tree you will need more soil, but if you plant herbaceous plants, less will do. Don't build berm right against the foundation of a house or on top of the roots of any mature tree. Building berms over tree roots will create a hazardous situation over time and greatly impact the health of the trees.

A few helpful tips for you to build raised planting beds or a berm.

- Remove soil, lawn and other unwanted material from the spot where the berm will be placed. Make it flat.

- Break up the surface of the soil by digging. This will reduce the profile of compacted soil and assist drainage.

- Place well-drained sandy loam first, then clay loam and topsoil to finish the berm. Subsoil layer is the foundation of the berm, so pay attention when constructing it.

- The topsoil should be 6-12 inches thick on the top of the subsoil. Slightly (2-3 inches) mix the subsoil and the topsoil at the joint. This will ensure a proper drainage and integration of soils.

- Rake and tamp the berm down to settle the soil and reduce air pockets from it.

- The berm is ready to plant ground covers, trees, flowers or shrubs, but water it gently until the berm is stabilized and settled.

Building elevated areas such as raised beds and berms will give your garden character and added interest. It will allow you to plant that require decent drainage.

Landscaping in layers

Landscaping in layers may sound complicated, but it's an interesting concept in landscaping design and serves you well in several ways. In layer landscaping, you plant a wide variety of shrubs, herbaceous plants, bulbs, ground covers, trees and vines in your garden. This type of landscaping allows you to enjoy multiple seasons with various colors, textures and heights of different plants.

In addition to attractiveness, layer landscaping is healthy for plants. It creates an environment where plants benefit from one another. For example, offering one another shelter and shade. A diverse ecosystem is likely to survive environmental challenges such as extreme weather, heat, drought, climate change and pests.

Few tips for layer landscaping

- Choose a variety of plants for your garden that prefer similar growing conditions, such as light, moisture, soil and climate.

- Plant the low plants in front of the garden, medium-height plants in the middle part and tallest trees in the back of the garden. If your garden can be viewed from all sides, plant the tallest trees in the middle and work down from there according to plant heights.

- Plant a variety of plants, but don't overcrowd them.

- Use a balanced combination of small, medium and tall plants together with other qualities such as blooming times, fruit or fall foliage.

- Plant only native plants in truly native wooded areas.

Effective watering techniques for a healthy, lush, low cost landscaping

The smart and low-maintenance way to manage water in your garden is to use new and efficient watering devices such as drip irrigation, rotor and misting sprinkler heads/ soaker hoses. Water efficient drip systems or soaker hoses will save water and make your life a lot easier. Let's discuss few effective watering systems

- Drip irrigation: Micro-irrigation or drip irrigation systems are among the most effective and efficient ways to supply plants with water. Micro-irrigation is a watering technique that supplies small amounts of water drip to plant roots thru a system of tubing, pipes, emitters and valves. You can use drip irrigation in vegetable gardens, shrub borders, flower beds, hanging baskets and containers.

- Soaker Hoses: Soaker hoses are basically porous hoses that are attached to a garden faucet or hose to evenly distribute water to the plants. You can place soaker hoses under a thin layer of mulch or on the surface. Soaker hoses come in handy when watering flower beds, trees, shrubs or vegetable gardens.

- Rotary and Mister: Rotary sprinkler sprays a stream of water to a desired length and width. You can adjust and change the size of the head of the rotary to modify the angle, rotation and distribution of water. Misters also spray water, but they do not rotate like rotary sprinklers. Misters are better for smaller gardens.

Harvesting rainwater

You can collect rainwater in a 30-50 gallon barrel. Rain barrels save money and helps you to better utilize water. A wooden or plastic rain barrel is tied into the downspout by placing it exactly under the pipe.

When it rains, the rain water flows to the downspout and finally to the rain barrel. Usually there is a faucet at the base of the barrel, attach a garden hose to the faucet and use water as needed.

The barrel water can be gravity-fed or you can use pumps to distribute the water to the garden. Rain barrels are suitable for flower beds, houseplants, trees, shrubs, vegetable gardens and outdoor annual containers.

Grey water

Grey water is just wastewater generated from household uses such as baths, showers, dishwashers, sinks and washing machines. Toilet water doesn't include in grey water and it considered as black water.

You can simply collect grey water with a bucket and water lawns and plants with it. Grey water saves on energy and water bills. You can use grey water on shrubs, ornamental plants, trees and lawns.

A few recommendations when using grey water

- Don't use grey water on vegetable crops
- Avoid contact with leaves of plants and apply grey water directly to the soil
- Evenly distribute grey water over a large area of the garden, avoid steep hills
- Apply grey water in flower beds with mulch to absorb water quickly in the soil

- Don't use grey water on young plants and apply only on mature plants. Don't use on acid-loving plants such as azaleas, hollies and rhododendrons.

Improved watering equipment, rain harvesting methods, and utilizing gray water are all great ways to save and reduce water and maintain a low-cost landscaping.

Chapter - 5
GARDEN DESIGN: THE MAIN COMPONENTS

This book provides phenomenal, well researched, eco-friendly, designs that can apply to any country in the world and any size of garden. Besides the fact that they can transform your desolate yard into a tranquil, relaxing, functional and entertaining dream garden.

Without further ado, here is a list of what garden design entails:

- Basic Elements of Landscape Design

- Materials

- Planning the Garden

- Drawing Up A Plan

Basic Elements of Landscape Design

These rudiments showcase the simplicity and artistic nature of lavishly striking, serene outdoor refuge drenched with color by blending them appropriately. Nonetheless when used in a synchronized manner, they are able to conceal les pleasing aspects, create privacy and correspondingly create the illusion of space.

Line

As a rule of thumb, this is one of the bare essentials of design. It determines how plant groupings fit or flow. Curved lines convey a feeling of lingering and free movement; straight lines such as pavements encourage movement and direct attention to a focal look while vertical lines enhance height. By way of example, careful selection of positioning of such verticals as fences, hedges, garden structures, trees and shrubs alter height by generating effects like screening (hide particular objects) and framing (draw attention to particular objects e.g. buildings).

Color

When properly orchestrated, by following the color wheel effectively, the best possible harmony is achieved. Moreover, color brings variety and personality. As a matter of fact, calm colors move away from you while warm colors bring things closer.

Visually, a garden should be a feast of colors which doesn't necessarily mean an overly vibrant and full-on-design incorporating every color under the sun. Don't overdo color to avoid being fed up with visual dis -agreement. On the other hand, a restrained, purely verdant garden can be the most relaxing scheme enveloped within the resting color.

Form

It encompasses different shapes and sizes of your plants, hardscapes or garden structures, which create natural groupings. In other words, trees with upright growth allow placement near structures, spreading trees as magnificent oak are ideal for shade while oval or rounded shrubs provide a uniform, symmetrical appearance and are often planted in front of a house.

Scale

This is the proportion in landscape. The size of plants and structures should balance in relation to each other and the space you are landscaping while still maintaining a comfortable environment (smooth, flowing appearance)

Materials

First and foremost, materials should be of one or two different textures to prevent the garden from looking too busy. They should blend in terms of color, texture and dimensions. Aside from that, they should relate to the style and finish of the house. Either you could build walls, patios, paths and raised beds using same brick throughout or a combination of brick and stone or make all the vertical structures such as fences and screens from the same wood or in one particular style–perhaps rustic.

The different types of materials are:

Paving

Natural Stone- Very good looking and may echo stone of surrounding building. Despite this, they can be quite heavy, expensive and sometimes slippery when wet. Limestone and travertine- Likewise looks great but may take on moisture and are susceptible to frost damage.

Slabs- Not only do they come in a variety of shapes including hexagonal, octagonal and circular but pre-cast slabs are also cheap. The downside is that they are brittle and break easily.

Concrete- It is used as a final finish. Better yet it is versatile to infill most spaces. The negative aspect is that it may look dull thus it may use in conjunction with another material e.g. brick edging.

Bricks- They are lovely and can be laid in interesting patterns such as herringbone, shelter or basket weave. However since they are dark, they may be unsuitable for small shady garden.

Decking- A very warm, quiet, free-draining material that is extremely versatile which comes in a great variety of natural patterns and colors. On top of that it particularly combines well with gravel, plants and water. In respect to that wood should be well treated to avoid slippery and rot.

Slate- Quite interesting when used except for the fact that it can be dark, dominating and slippery when wet.

Gravel, Pebbles, Granite Sets- Usually they are very versatile and they can be laid on sand or cement bed. Better yet they are most suited to courtyards that do not need to be completely leveled.

Tiles- Either they are made of ceramic or terracotta. More importantly, they should be frost-proof, non-slippery and thick enough not to crack if something is dropped on them. To be precise, a minimum of 10mm thick.

Metal Grids- E.g. galvanized steel grids can be 'floated' over areas to let light through a basement below.

Planning the garden

The most fascinating aspect of gardening is that every exclusive, smart yard is unique because every owner is also unique. Additionally, there are two critical areas to be considered, the front and back yard. The front yard makes the first impression thus should be inspiring, well thought and consistent with the style of your home e.g. a low maintenance flower garden.

The backyard is mostly for entertainment and play time forthwith carries most of the structures and multifunctional features. Therefore you can incorporate seating, dining areas or sunny relaxation spots. For the ultimate party house, you may choose to incorporate a pool and a patio or a deck with a fire pit, outdoor fireplace, barbecue or an outdoor kitchen.

Steps in planning

1. Draw up a list of what you want from the garden. Don't also forget to take into account the needs and wishes of the other family members in relation to the garden.

2. Access the space. Pay attention to the size, the direction it faces, effects of neighboring buildings or trees, or the amount of sun or shade it receives, the presence of damp or exposed spots and the type of soil.

3. Zoning the garden. This is the areas where you want to put specific features. (Some are

moved, removed or added). Keep in mind the need for ease of access around the garden and safety.

Some features you may need to take into account include;

- Utility; Paths, storage for cars and bicycles, compost bin, lighting, washing line and greenhouse.

- Recreation; Patio, recreation, lawn, barbecue, play area, and water features.

- Ornamental; Trees, shrubs, roses, raised beds and bog gardens.

Drawing Up A Plan

Firstly, it is fundamental to measure the garden accurately and draw a scale plan. A scale plan is simply an overhead view of the garden reduced to a size convenient for you to copy onto a sheet of paper. As an illustration, if children's play area is needed, it should not be located in a faraway corner where the children cannot be watched over.

Most plans are drawn to a scale of 1:50 or 1:100. For instance for the 1:50 scale, every dimension you measure in the garden such as the length of a fence is divided by 50 before being drawn on the plan. Therefore a 30 ft. (10m) long fence would be 8 inch (20cm) on the plan.

Chapter – 6
PLANT DESIGN OVERVIEW

Where does one start when choosing the plant material for the gardens?

Ideally, by the time you are ready to choose your plants; the various patios, walkways, lawn areas, pool and spa and other yard features have already had their locations determined, and the empty spaces left to be filled with plants have been defined. This gives you an idea of how many plants you will need.

After the patios were laid out, this garden was designed to feature lots of color contrast.

Of course, if you have a wide working knowledge of locally available trees and shrubs, along with their particular growth characteristics, you could just sit down and fill in the spaces on your drawing with plants of various sizes that fit well in those blank areas on your paper or your computer screen. I have found, however, in the real world that this is not necessarily the approach that yields the best result, even when being tackled by a professional designer with a lot of experience. And going on the assumption that most people reading this book are not already garden-design professionals, here is the process, one step at a time.

The overall purpose is to achieve a beautiful garden design by putting together a great combination of plants that will all thrive in a particular environment. This is the positive goal. As mentioned earlier, though, we can look at it more as a process of elimination. Approached this way, the field of choices gets narrowed down each step of the way, lessening the number of choices which need to be made as it goes along. Thinking of it and handling it this way, one choice at a time, is a good way to get steady progress.

We already touched on the need to consider

any screening requirements. If this applies to your yard, it is probably a good place to start. You can take note of where you might need large screening material and jot this on your plan.

Along with this, any particular items that you already know you want can be noted down as well—particularly any plant features that will take up a fair amount of space. Perhaps you have always wanted a couple of fruit trees, for instance, or a grouping of roses. These will be among your key features and as each one is added to your drawing, more of the garden space will be used up. You may not know yet exactly which trees or plants you will use, but you will be determining how many plant items to look for and of what general type.

You should get some idea of what kind of soil you have, just in a very general way. Mostly you are interested in how well it drains. Sandy soils tend to drain very well and heavy clay soil can hold water for a very long time. If you can't tell easily; one trick is to dig a hole, perhaps 18 inches deep, and fill it with water. If it drains within a couple of hours or less, you can consider that you have good drainage. If it just sits there overnight and takes a few days to go away, you likely have a lot of clay.

This data will allow you to possibly eliminate

some of the plants you look at as you consider all the choices available. Many plants specify good drainage in the soil for optimum growth. If you have heavy clay, you can either cross those plants off the list as you run across them, or at least know that those plants will likely need extra soil preparation work and probably special care if you do decide to use them.

Checking the direction that the sun moves across the sky in relationship to your yard will give you an idea of which garden areas will have more shade and which will be in the sun most of the day. The afternoon sun is much more of a factor than the morning sun, which tends to be a lot milder. This will give you an idea of how many sun loving-plants you will need versus how many shade tolerant ones should end up on your list. It isn't a bad idea to just check the shade patterns in the yard a few times during the day, and note this on your drawing so you don't have to remember it later. Keep in mind when you do this that the summer sun rides higher in the sky and presents a different shade pattern than other times of the year. The shade and sun areas during the summer months are the most important to consider.

If you live in an area that is subject to frost, snow, or high winds, you may want to take note of these factors. This will speed up your search for the right plants by allowing you to eliminate those that will be more trouble than they are worth.

These plants were all selected from available material at local nurseries.

Armed with this information, almost certainly the best step to take next is to go see what is out there. Even after designing plants for years we still do this from time to time. Taking a few trips out to some local nurseries, or home improvement stores before filling in the garden areas on your plan can be a huge help in more ways than one. It lets you know what is actually available, so you aren't specifying things on your plan you won't be able to get for one reason or another. Also, just strolling through a nursery can give you a lot of ideas as you simply come across things that you like.

This prolific yellow rose is named after Henry Fonda, the actor. In fact, this one is planted right outside my office window.

Many nurseries that cater to the retail market, and particularly home improvement stores, have tags on each plant that give you information such as how big the plant grows, what kind of soil it likes, how much sun or shade it can take and what kind of water requirement it has. Take a note pad with you so you can jot down the characteristics of each plant you think you might want to use. This can make your life a lot easier later when you plot out the final design.

If you want to really see how the plants look together, you can stack various plants in groups on your cart as you walk around the nursery and get a good feel of how the various colors and textures look together.

Snapping photos and taking notes could give you a handy reference tool to use when you begin adding the plants to your design drawing. You can quickly decide if a particular plant should go in the shady or sunny part of the yard. It can help you group plants together that like a lot of water so the sprinklers can be set up to water those areas more than the garden areas that have drought-tolerant plants.

This springtime mountainside look actually contains low water-requirement plants.

There are lots of little reasons you may want this information at your fingertips. For example, perhaps you want a citrus tree, but the only place it will fit in the yard is in one of the lawn areas. Citrus trees don't like to be kept wet all the time, and actually won't produce fruit well if kept this way. However, it can work if you mound the area where the tree is planted so that the excess water drains away. If you have notes handy on the various requirement of each different plant, you can use them to make decisions like this as your drawing progresses, paying attention to one plant at a time.

When you are done with your trips to the nurseries, you now have all the ingredients for your garden recipe at your fingertips.

When this ground cover (Verbena Tapien) is in bloom, it is quite stunning.

In addition to making your plant list, there are a few more reasons for using this mobile approach to plant designing. For one thing, it can be a lot of fun. Casually wandering through nurseries is probably one of the least stressful activities available anywhere in the world and can be a good thing to do just for its own sake. This has a practical side, too, in that it can take you out, away from your drawing table and allow your creativity to soar.

Also, if the plants are actually for sale in your area, chances are they will do well in your local climate. This information might be available in a reference book, but those tend to contain far too many choices and working only from reference books will probably just lead to confusion. These books also tend to cover very large geographic areas, and micro climates are quite common. If a plant is available in your local nursery it usually means that particular plant will live in your area.

Looking at the actual plants also gives you the advantage of being able to feel the texture of the leaves, smell any scent they give off and see what the color of the flowers actually are.

There are lots of colors and textures to choose from in designing the plants for a garden.

I should also note that there have been times when we have been presented with a (usually expensive) blueprint by a homeowner that was drawn by an architect that didn't involve the owner in the actual, physical details of the plant choices. Since the plants all have Latin names, often the property owner really didn't know what he or she was getting. Last minute changes on plans like this are very common once the details of the various plants are made known to the homeowner. Most of the installation work we have done is based on our own designs (which do involve the owner in the details during the design process) so we haven't had this problem ourselves, but it is a good example of why the hands-on design process is the best approach overall. Usually we do the hands-on work at the nurseries for our clients, and use photographs to discuss design possibilities, but it is not uncommon for us to meet the client at a nursery and just stroll around, doing exactly what we are talking about here.

Searching the nurseries in the local area can turn up all sorts of interesting plant choices.

Another reason for seeing what's out there before spending the time to finalize your design is that some of the plants picked out of a book might not be readily available. Just like any other store, the nurseries have to decide what to stock and they won't have it all. If you see what they already have first, you don't need to change your design due to availability issues. Designing most of your choices from what you already know is available will save you a ton of aggravation.

Chapter - 7
TREES AND FLOWERS FOR YOUR LANDSCAPING DESIGN

MANGO (Mangifera Indica):

 A large evergreen tree with a dense dome shaped crown of leaves, reaching up to 20m in height. Trunk: Straight, with dark grey rough bark, cracks when old. Leaves: Oblong lanceolate wavy leaves of size 4-5 cm with shining margins crowded at ends of branches. Flowers: Yellowish-white, small in dense clusters, larger than leaves, fragrant in January - March. Fruit: Large, fleshy, April - June. Wild in mixed deciduous forests but mainly cultivated for its luscious fruit both by farmers and householders. It is considered

to be an auspicious tree.

NEEM / MARGOSA (Azadichata Indica):

A large, evergreen tree up to 15 m tall, having a dark grey bark with long and oblique fissures on the outer surface. Leaves: Alternate; Each leaflet oblique, lanceolate with toothed margin, slightly bitter in taste. Flowers: Whitish, honey scented, large number of bees. Fruit: Greenish yellow of size approx. 1 cm, egg-like oval, relished by birds. One of the commonest trees in India though a native of Burma. Considered a sacred and health giving tree chiefly because of insecticidal and medicinal properties. Deep rooted suited for desert or semi-arid land.

PAGODA TREE (Plumeria Rubra):

The tree is small and gouty looking, often leafless but rarely out of bloom. Leaves: grow in crowded 'spiral' at the tips of the branches exceeding 30 cm, smooth broadly lance-shaped, tapering at both ends. Veins are distinctive and straight. Leaves fall off during November-December. Flowers: Fragrant flowers in upright clusters at the tips of branches. White and pink varieties are common. Fruit: Pods in pairs, about 12 cm long. This tree is grown in warm parts of India and generally cultivated as an ornamental tree.

MOHWA (Madhuca Indica):

A deciduous medium sized tree, having up to 15 cm thick trunk, with a short bole and numerous branches forming a thick leafy crown. Bark dark colored, cracked, exuding milky latex. Leaves: Clustered near the ends of branches. It is leathery, elliptic and hairy when young. Flowers: Pendulous, in dense clusters at the ends of branches, calyx rusty, and corolla creamy, fleshy, edible sweet. A good tree may yield 200kg of petals per year. Fruit: Fleshy, ovoid berry, densely rusty, 4-5 cm in diameter having 1-4 seeds. The tree is commonly grown in the Indian plains; cultivated near rural settlements for flowers and seeds which are rich in oil.

MAHARUK (MAHANIMB) (Ailanthus Excelsa):

A large, deciduous tree of up to 30 m height having a light grey intact bark. Leaves: Imparipinate, 25-50 cm long with 8-14 pairs of leaflets which are variable in shape. Each leaflet 10-15 cm, lance shaped oblique at base. It smells bitter. Flowers: Small and yellowish in large lax bunches. Fruit: Flat pod like, brown, winged 3-5 * 1cm. Tapering at both ends, twisted at base. A graceful tree occurring in deciduous forests, often planted at roadsides.

JAVA FIG (Ficus Comosa):

A hardy medium sized fig tree with slender hanging roots. The roots do not form columns or props as in the banyan and so the tree does not spread as much. Leaves: Glossy, leathery, broadly ovate, which look graceful on drooping branches. Flowers: Inconspicuous, contained inside the immature figs; mainly in March-April. Fruit: In form of figs about the size of pea, smooth, yellowish green with purplish spots. It is Relished by birds and often cultivated as an avenue tree.

INDIAN LABURNUM (Cassia Fistula):

A medium sized deciduous tree reaching up to 10m, bark smooth and ash colored in young trees. It is rough and dark brown in old trees. Leaves: Compound, pinnate, 20-40cm long bearing 4-8 pairs of leaflets. Each leaflet 4-9cm, smooth, bright green above and Covered with silvery hair below. New leaves appear between April-may, the tree being leafless in Feb-march. Flowers: Arranged in drooping racemes 30-45cm long bearing bright yellow, fragrant bunch of flowers with some resemblance to the English laburnum. Fruit: Straight, cylindrical pods, 3D-100cm about 2-3cm in diameter. It becomes smooth, green turning dark brown with age. It is common in deciduous forests allover India up to 1500m. Various parts of the tree are used in indigenous medicine. Golden yellow patches of flowers when the forest is almost leafless.

GULMOHAR (Delonix Regia):

One of the most popular, quick growing, deciduous tree, reaching up to 15m. Bark slightly rough, grayish brown, branches spreading. Leaves: Feathery, bipinnate, up to 60cm long, composed of 11-18 pinnae. Each pinna bears 20-30 pairs of small oblong leaflets, dancing with breeze. Flowers: Appear with the onset of hot weather and the whole tree is a blaze of scarlet bloom in April-may. Flowers are found in immense clusters at the ends of branches. One of the petals is slightly larger and variegated in Color. It is chiefly pollinated by birds. Fruit: Pods flat, 30-60 cm long, green when young, harden with age, turn deep brown and remain for a long time on the tree. The seeds are oblong and transversely mottled. A native of Madagascar, it had been introduced to India and grown through the tropics.

CORAL JASMINE (Nyctanthes Arbortristis):

A small tree up to 10m high. Branches quadrangular, Covered with stiff white hair. Leaves: Opposite, ovate, entire or with a few large and distant teeth, 9-14 * 7cm, upper surface rough with bulbous hair, lower surface with addressed hair. Flowers: In terminal pyramidal bunches; fragrant, white with coral-orange tube. August - December. Forest bloom during the night and fall off in the morning. Fruit: A capsule, flat, obcordate, 1–6 cm across with 2 seeds. It is indigenous in North, North-East and Central India. It is widely cultivated for its fragrant flowers. Corolla was formerly used for dyeing silk.

CHAMPAK (Michelia Champaca):

A tall stately evergreen tree usually up to 10-12m high. It is sometimes reaching 30m as in the Himalayan foothills. Trunk straight with greenish brown bark, branches ascending to form a dense crown.

Leaves: Smooth, leathery, crate, lance shaped. It is slightly hairy on the lower side, 5-8 cm on a stalk, which is grooved. Flowers: Golden yellow 5-6 cm in size with sweet intoxicating fragrance arising singly from the axils of leaves. April-September. Fruits: A cluster of woody, ovoid fruits containing angular seeds with brown or pink covering usually planted for fragrant flowers and as an ornamental tree in gardens.

YELLOW OLEANDER (Thevetia Peruviana):

A small tree, normally up to 5 m with many branches, milky, with smooth trunk, often knotted. Leaves: Narrow, linear, 2-7 cm, smooth, shiny above, dull green below arising in whorls. Flowers: Yellow; bell shaped, fragrant, 4-5 cm long, almost throughout the year. Fruits: Greenish, smooth like a jointed pebble. It is usually cultivated near temples or households. It thrives best in sun, easily Propagated by cuttings. All parts toxic avoided by cattle.

Flowering Annuals

1. COMMON NAME: Aster

BOTANICAL NAME: Callistephus chinensis

NATURAL ORDER: Composite

PLANTING DISTANCE: 8-10inches

METHOD OF PROPAGATION: transplanted

HEIGHT: 1-2.5ft.

COLOR: except yellow all colors.

2. COMMON NAME: Calendula

BOTANICAL NAME: Calendula afficialis

NATURAL ORDER: Compositae

PLANTING DISTANCE: 8-12inches

METHOD OF PROPAGATION: transplanted

HEIGHT: 1-1.5ft.

COLOR: Yellow or orange.

3. COMMON NAME: Candytuft

BOTANICAL NAME: Iberis umbillat

NATURAL ORDER: Curciferae

PLANTING DISTANCE: 6-8inches

METHOD OF PROPAGATION: transplanted

HEIGHT: 8-12inches.

COLOR: Pure white and rose purple.

4. COMMON NAME: Pansy

BOTANICAL NAME: Viola tricolor

NATURAL ORDER: Violacae

PLANTING DISTANCE: 2-4inches

METHOD OF PROPAGATION: transplanted

HEIGHT: 6-8inches.

COLOR: flowers of different shades and combinations.

5. COMMON NAME: Phlox

BOTANICAL NAME: Phlox drummondi

NATURAL ORDER: Polemoniaceae

PLANTING DISTANCE: 8-10 inches

METHOD OF PROPAGATION: transplanted

HEIGHT: 6-12 inches.

COLOR: All colors and bicolors.

Chapter - 8
THE SOCIAL AND SMALL CITY GARDEN DESIGN

Social Garden Design

For those who enjoy entertaining guests, a social garden design is ideal. This design takes into consideration privacy above all else. The best way to provide such privacy not only for yourself, your family, and your guests, is to plant trees and plants called "climbers" to form a natural screen. If you opt for trees, be sure to avoid planting them too close to your home or that of any neighbor because the roots can, with time, damage your foundation. You can, alternatively, place trees at the end of the garden area to form a screen which does not hinder the view you have from your home.

Once you have established your privacy, you need to create a seating area. You might consider a deck and built in future. This can be very sleek, customized to your garden theme or tastes, and is typically weatherproof. Weatherproof furniture is an important component. If you are going to build a deck and add outdoor furniture to this design, you want to measure the amount of shade and sunlight your garden area receives. You will have to keep track of where the sun falls throughout the day and where the warmth will be. When dining, for example, people tend to prefer shade. If your yard is sunny most of the time with no naturally shaded area, you will need to plant something that creates shade, like a row of tall bushes which form a screen. Under this screen, you can place your outdoor dining furniture.

Be practical about the design. If you want to include a dining area, for example, you might not have room to include a garden shed. This means that your gardening tools will need a new home. In such cases, try to think practically: use seats or design a table that has a lid on top and doubles as a tabletop workbench. This allows you a place to store your garden tools discreetly while you are entertaining.

When it comes to seating look for comfort no matter the design you want. Invest money in seat cushions which are weatherproof. Guests will want someplace soft to sit and relax when you bring them outside. Investing in seat cushions means extending the longevity of your outdoor furniture but can easily be thrown in the wash if they get too dirty.

If you decide to have an outdoor deck, one that is raised, you will need to visually soften the edges. This does not mean you have to change the outdoor deck design, but rather, leave the deck protruding and cover the borders with different plants. The best plans to use our scented herbs or fresh herbs because they will not only visually soften the social garden design, they smell great, and if you are cooking outside and simply pick one or two fresh herbs to sprinkle on top of your dishes.

As a finishing touch to your social garden design, consider adding trellises around your dining area. Trellises offer a very coordinated and neat appearance. They are also easier amended than old fences. Perhaps best of all is the fact that you can train scented climbing plants to grow up the trellis like Jasmine. This not only gives you a private escape that is aesthetically appealing but offers a wonderful aroma.

Walkways Increase Accessibility

Adding a walkway to the garden design offers multiple advantages. First and perhaps most obvious is your garden becomes more accessible. Second, you increase your ability to move around from one place to the next without stumbling upon uneven ground or tripping over a delicate flower. For social garden designs, you will have many guests traipsing around your garden and if you have walkways you can insist that all guests stick to the walkway so that they do not harm any of your vulnerable, valuable, or rare plants. You can protect your garden investments while still granting your guests access to your design.

Another benefit to walkways, especially a wooden walkway, is the wheelchair accessibility. If you have a friend or family member who is confined to a wheelchair, you can make a wonderful and memorable evening out by offering them the chance to enjoy your garden.

Patios

For your social garden design, if you are hosting outdoor cookouts for parties you might consider incorporating the patio for additional accessibility and functionality. Figure out what you want the patio to be used for and that will help you figure out the size. A small space which is roughly 8' x 8' is perfect if you just want to cook but not necessarily seat all of your guests on the patio. There are many shapes available including rectangular and square shapes for attractive patio designs. Squares are obviously the more traditional route.

If you create your small patio you can use bricks, tiles, or landscaping stones or the design. This is perfect if you plan on having any type of seating area and need a level surface on which to place your furniture. If you already have a patio you can accent the area with a pergola or a gazebo.

With regard to the materials available for your patio, concrete is durable and easily customizable. You can change the color before you mix the concrete but it can only be poured in good weather and can be expensive. Paving stones are a more attractive option that is reasonably priced but in order for you to use paving stones, you have to prepare the area by making it level. Brick is great because of the starting performance and variety of color options. The only downside with brick is that the site, much like with paving stones, have to be prepared ahead of time so that each brick fit snugly with those bricks around it. Gravel is the final choice available in multiple sizes, styles, and colors. It's very affordable but if your patio is being used for dining, gravel will provide a sturdy surface for your furniture.

Small City Garden Design

For those of you who live in a city and have a very small space, do not fret. You can make a small city garden that provides you with utility, privacy, and feels much bigger than it is.

The design for a small city garden has to be very well organized so that it delivers not only the degree of privacy that a city dweller will need, ample seating opportunities for guests but structural plants and style. The result will be a space that truly encapsulates a vibrant energy in which you can relax after a long day in the city.

Seating is one of the most important considerations for a small city garden design. The most significant feature you will find in any small garden is a very attractive table and a matching bench set. The reason for this is quite simple. That piece of furniture becomes the focal point. So it doubles as a structural device and a place for seating. As such it is important to make sure it is as attractive as possible.

Beyond the seating, you can create a great screen with role bamboo trees or all of the trees. This not only creates a strong structural presence in your garden but it acts as a boundary. The repetition created by a row of trees seamlessly blending into the rest of your garden creates a sense of harmony.

You will need a small footpath more than likely from your back door or side door to the seating area in the garden. Along this path, you should have low plants. These low plants will help offset a bigger paved region that a city garden usually has and it brings the green color much closer to the area of the garden you will use the most. If you don't have room for a large lawn or you simply cannot care for one, you can try a low maintenance gravel surface. This will also give you a space for extra seating opportunities. If you feel so inclined you can blend paving stones with different granite chips to add some variety in this space in lieu of a traditional lawn.

Chapter - 9
LANDSCAPE STYLES FOR DIFFERENT ENVIRONMENT

Landscape Designs for Tropical Areas

The best landscape styles for gardens located in tropical regions are the rustic and low-maintenance styles. This is because the plants required to achieve these styles are appropriate for the tropical climate. You won't have to spend time taking care of these plants since they can readily survive in your area.

The Rustic Style

- The plants you need to achieve a rustic landscape are: ferns, vine maple, different varieties of elderberry (e.g. Madonna, Black Lance, Common Native, Black Beauty, etc.), as well as ninebark plants (e.g. Native, Center glow, Diabolo, Coppertiana, etc.)

- Get these plants if you want to add a meadow-like feel to your rustic garden:

- Penstemon

- Echiracea plant

- ox-eye daisies

- Rudbeckia nitida plant

- Morning light grass

When using this style, you should try to reflect on the appearance of the natural environment. This principle is particularly important for gardens found in grasslands or woodlands. However, although this kind of style needs to show a "natural" look, you need to know some basic guidelines. These are:

What you should do:

a) Utilize pathways to create "mood-changing" effects – It is best if you will use a wide pathway for the entry point of your garden because it encourages the visitor to quickly walk into the area. The pathway should become narrower inside the garden to slow the person down and let him/her appreciate the landscape.

b) Allow the moss to grow – Moss provides a unique feel to the structures of a rustic landscape. Professionals consider it as excellent addition to this style.

What you should not do:

a) Do not use plants that are available everywhere – You want your landscape to be unique, so stay away from generic garden plants. You may start your own plant collection by checking the ferns and herbs found in your region. Afterwards, include plants that will provide additional texture and multicolored foliage.

Low Maintenance Landscape Design

- The plant choices – you have to focus on plants that can survive with minimal care. Hardy evergreen plants are the usual choices of professional landscape artists. When selecting the plants to use, always check their average height and range of foliage. Avoid plants that tend to spread out too wide because you will be required to prune them regularly.

- To achieve a great looking low maintenance landscape, you just have to avoid a few things. These are:

a) Mature plants – You may attempt to establish your garden instantly by buying mature plants, but this option often causes maintenance problems. It is best to start your garden with younger plants since they usually require minimal attention.

b) Delicate plants – If you have these plants in your landscape, you will need to move, wrap, and relocate them on a regular basis. This will require time and effort from you, which is against the core principle of the low maintenance style.

Landscape Styles for Cold Regions

Cold climate is great for whimsical and wild styles of landscaping.

The Whimsical Style

When using this style, you need to look for things that can be "repurposed" (e.g. toilets, bathtubs, etc.) They can be used as containers for your plants, and will give your landscape an unusual and interesting effect.

You can also include old garden equipment into your landscape. For example, you can place a beat-up wheelbarrow in one of the corners of your garden and use it as a container for your plants or flowers.

The Wild Style

To ensure that your wild landscape gets everyone's attention, you must use brightly colored flowers and plants with different sizes and textures. Your best options are: peonies, lobelias, boxwood, lavenders and irises.

The only rule that you have to keep in mind is this: always check the height of plants before adding them into your garden. This is important since you are going to use the landscape to create privacy.

Landscape Designs for Dry Areas

Beautiful gardens can be established even in regions with high temperatures and minimal water availability. We will focus on the Desert and Tuscan landscape styles.

Desert Landscape Style

In this landscape design, you should use succulents and plants that are accustomed to hot temperatures. The plants commonly used in this style are:

- Agave

- Cacti

- Sedum

- Aloe

- Yucca

Here are some colorful plants that can survive in your region: yellow columbine, begonia, bunny ears, and autumn sage. You should never attempt to have a lawn when doing this style since that requires regular supply of water.

Tuscan Design

This particular style combines popular plants (e.g. rosemary, lavender, Italian cypress, etc.) and brightly colored items (e.g. natural stones, flowers, and urns).

Here are the plants commonly used by professionals:

- Thyme
- Fig
- Bay
- Citrus
- Olive
- Grape vine
- Italian cypress
- Rosemary

- Lavender

Grasses used as ornaments in the Tuscan style are:

- Moor
- Lindheimer's muhly
- Deer grass

Landscape artists sometimes add these to Tuscan gardens:

- Pearl blue bush
- Mediterranean fan
- Different varieties of sage (e.g. bee's bliss, white, Jerusalem, and Cleveland sages).

Landscape Designs for Areas with Moderate Climate

This chapter will focus on the French and Colonial styles of landscaping.

The French Style

When using this style in designing your landscape, you need to include these basic elements:

- Glazed pots
- Fountains
- Concrete balustrade
- Birdbaths
- Antique ornaments
- Natural stones
- Elegant furniture
- Iron seats
- Columns
- Trellises

To ensure that your French garden catches the attention of everyone, keep these things in mind:

Geometry – In designing your garden, everything should be geometric and positioned symmetrically.

Terraces – should be positioned in the garden so that every detail of the landscape can be easily viewed.

1.3 Water – is considered as the primary element of this style. Use pools and fountains in oval, rectangular, or circular shapes.

Chapter - 10
THE GARDEN COUNTRY STYLE

The garden in country style is ideal for small country sites. Its main features are fruit trees, berry bushes, lush flower beds of the front garden and absolute undemanding care. That's why the country garden is the most practical of all existing species. But at the same time - it's a great place to relax. Recreate the country style in the landscape design of your own site is not at all difficult, but the very design of the garden requires a developed sense of proportion and good taste - it is not worth overdoing the details.

His founder was the world-famous design expert and professional artist Gertrude Jackkil. The basis of the style were popular in the old days of cottage gardens in England, Gertrude gave the gardens aesthetics and created picturesque compositions.

Gertrude Jackkil opened the untouched beauty of refined gardens to the world. Europe gladly accepted this innovation, according to the projects of a talented designer, more than 350 objects in rural country style were broken up. The popularity of the direction was more influenced by the simplicity of caring for the garden, and little by little, taking the basics, each people contributed to the development of the style.

The country garden, although it should look slightly neglected, but must have certain zones, attributes and be created according to its own special principles.

Romanticism

A popular garden in the country style always looks romantic - and all thanks to the abundance of flowers. Exotics in it will be inappropriate, but hydrangeas, phlox, peonies, jasmine and lilacs - just fit. You can even plant plants that do not require any care: chamomile, yarrow, cornflower, plantain and many others.

Easy Negligence

In the country garden, categorically cannot be either perfectly cut lawns, or too smooth paths - everything should look like the garden itself is just a piece of the surrounding nature. For the same reason, it is impossible to use any synthetic materials or bright plastic figurines in such a garden. But clay pots, wooden watering cans and old wheels from carts will fit into this in garden design in the style of the country as well as possible.

Accessories That Convey the Spirit of the Garden

To create a real garden in the country style, you need to put your soul into it. Therefore, it is in the country of stylization that you can, as much as you like, apply imagination - this style cannot be spoiled by a single new stroke.

In the country garden, as an accessory, the old wheels from the cart, which can be found through acquaintances in the village or buy decorative ones in a special store, are the first ones. Even better is to install a decorative small mill or even a whole wooden cart, and plant bright flowers in it.

Dwarfs for the garden can be brought, of course. But only they should harmoniously fit into the environment and not be too bright. But solar lanterns in their hands can be attached - then in the evenings in the garden will be incredibly fabulous.

Good humor and rural simplicity

Humor in the creation of your own hands country garden is simply necessary. And in order to add to its summer residence ironic notes, you only need:

1. Plant flower beds in large troughs, watering cans and wheelbarrows. So, as if these objects were abandoned here not less than a hundred years ago.

2. Sew and make cute garden stuffed animals and put them in different corners of the garden - as if they had been standing here all their life.

3. Acquire figures of animals or dwarfs and settle these wonderful inhabitants of the garden throughout the cottage area. So, as if only bearded men behind this garden and take care - there is no one else.

White fence and wattle fence with sunflowers

As a fence, you can put a real wattle fence, if the country is chosen by the Russian interpretation, or establish a beautiful dazzling white fence, like the Americans. Both will look great. But you can combine wood with a stone - also a good option.

And not necessarily the fence itself should be impressive and only from 2 meters in height. On the contrary, in creating a landscape design in the country style, you need to get as close to the village type of garden arrangement as possible. And their fences are always more conditional than those carrying a protective function - cute wooden fences with clay pots on top, a wattle fence with sunflowers and even just planted berry bushes.

Fragrant Berries and Fruit Trees

Mandatory elements of the country garden are berry bushes and fruit trees. This garden is especially beautiful in the spring, when cherry and apple blossom. In summer, currants, raspberries and gooseberries not only perfectly fit in the overall concept of the garden, but also pleasing with a pleasant sweet aroma. Not bad will be planted on the site and barberry, and viburnum, and aronia, which looks great in living hedges and bring a lot of fruit. And, of course, the classic lilac with jasmine - the smells of the garden will be unforgettable.

But there is one secret in the arrangement of the country garden: all plants and trees need to be selected so that they bloom at various times of the year, and then the villa site will please the eye for a year.

Bench near The House and Country Arbor

Benches by the house and a variety of gazebos for guests are obligatory elements of a country garden. And the older and shabby will be the furniture, the better. Today, even you can order from designers' artificial aging of new furniture - indeed, using real antiques is not even safe: an old beautiful chair can collapse under a guest at the most unexpected moment. And so for the country-interior and country-garden in Europe, it is customary to order "aging under country"

in design studios and workshops. To create the effect of antiquity, special paints, varnishes and skins go into the course - and a new table and chair for the garden looks as if it is already 100 years old, but durable, just as it was from the factory.

Ideal, of course, for such a garden wicker furniture, and if it is painted white, it will acquire a refined visual ease and sophistication.

But garden-style gazebos in the country style can be the most unusual - and in the form of a mill, and in the form of an old village house, and with decorative wheels.

Paths with Watering Cans and Flowers

The paths in the country garden can be made of any kind - the main thing is to use only natural materials for their backfilling. But along the paths you can safely make a live border of bright colors or leave them overgrown. Among them, it is best to arrange decorative watering cans and wooden water buckets, in which flowers seem to have sprouted long ago. The main thing is that the paths are florid, and there were many of them - and for children the game in such a garden will be a real fairy-tale journey.

Garden fence

The ideal fencing for the village garden can be considered a wattle fence or fence. It is on it that cheerful little groups can hang bright spots. If the fence is already created, and the garden is only planned, then too modern material (metal profile, concrete forms, etc.) can be closed on the inside by tall shrubs and trees, weaving plants, decorating them as a hedge. Just do not land in even rows of thuja, cypresses and junipers. These "guests" are inappropriate in the rural landscape. But lilac, bird cherry and ashberry - it's the thing! And if you plant an elder, it will also scare off flies from your acres.

The gate is best to plan a wooden one. You can add massive metal lining, performing the role of jewelry; you can make a thread the top edge. The decor will depend on the overall look of your fence. The main thing is to preserve the shade of antiquity and even some primitiveness.

In the landscape design in the country style is appropriate old well. A wooden frame with water for irrigation will also give charm to such a garden. And also a small pond, overgrown with reeds and water lilies floating on the surface of the water. Construct a wall fountain and a small inclined drain, the water from which will drain into a simple wooden trough. On the adjacent territory near the pond place a swing and a gazebo for rest, made of natural materials.

You cannot do without a garden in a country garden. It looks in the form of small neat beds with dill, parsley, lettuce, green onions. The beds can have different shapes: form a circle, triangle, square or hexahedron. They can be decorated with calendula, marigolds, nasturtium, feverfew, making combined plantings, in the center of which to place a chard with multi-colored stems. Here you can place old items of everyday use from tin and wood, for example, watering cans and buckets.

Chapter - 11
MINE BLOWING LANDSCAPING IDEAS

Gravel and Path Stones

 Gravel can be used in driveways and passages or even to line your lawns. Pathways can be paved with all sorts of materials: river stones, pebbles, bricks, flagstones, concrete slabs, and many others. You can create a quaint little passageway with rustic charm and story book flair by letting the grass or weeds go wild and once it reaches the desired height, then plow a path through it. It is simple to do and even simpler to maintain. Dirt paths are also a cheap and simple idea for passageways. You can create mosaics and use different colored

stones, broken crockery, or other materials to make them appear more visually pleasing. They can be hand painted with natural images such as flowers, butterflies, fruits, and others. You can shape and order them in any way you want: slightly curving, spiraling, circular, or straight going. The important thing is they lead and get you to the destination where they are supposed to. Their purpose is not only limited to the practical. While being perfectly usable, they can be a form of aesthetic design that complements and enriches their background.

Archways and Entrances

The outside of the garden matters just as much as the outside especially in cases where it is completely enclosed and unseen from beyond your property line. Even from this vantage point however, points of beauty can still be created as hints to what one might discover within the walls. Gates and entrances can be as elaborate or simple as you prefer. They form the first visual impression upon entering your living space- lawns, gardens, and yards included. You can use doors or gates as entrances within the garden as well. When you have secret walled gardens, gates can be a good idea for added mystery. They can be made from wood, iron, steel, or any other metal alloy.

Archways are a way of creating the illusion of entrance into a confined area without the actual use of a swinging door or gate. They provide richly visually stimulating fodder while serving the purpose of being openings to the different

s of your landscape plan.

Stairs, Steps, and Levels

One way of adding dimension to one's outdoor living space is through adding levels, especially in sloping areas. A prime example is the famous rice terraces of Banaue in the Philippines. The natives utilize the land effectively by creating flat levels of land where they can plant their crops. Similarly, one can utilize sloping areas and keep ones gardens situated in higher or lower places. This could be part of the design element and can also serve as a separating method- one level for vegetables, another for herbs, a third for flowers, and so on. If one wants to use the illusion of height, you can create an effect similar to that of a wall of flowers, just by layering them up on a slope. Stairs offer a quaint way of getting from on level to the other. You can formally make concrete stairs, complete with banisters or you could go with a more natural look to blend in with the surroundings.

Connecting with Nature

Fountains and Waterworks

 A sure way to add interest in one's garden and to mimic the scenes in nature is to have a working waterworks system. You can have fountains in any size, with statues spouting water into a pool. You could have mini waterfalls or simulated streams which aside from being visually attractive, give off that gentle soothing sound of rushing water. You could make use of an underground spring or river by building a well. Aside from being a possible water source, it could be a thing of beauty as well.

Ponds and Bridges

One way of getting close to nature is to create

habitats for living creatures. One of the most commonly made is a fishpond. It is a great way to house your aquatic animal friends while creating little spots of attractive landscaping. If the pond or pool is big enough, one may even put in a bridge for better viewing and feeding of the fishes, and to get you from one side to the other. Having ponds is a good way of nourishing aquatic flora and fauna as well. You can have water lilies or lotuses to beautifully spruce up the surface of the pond or pool.

Animal Feeders, Habitats, and Baths

Aside from creating habitats, another way of attracting animal life is by creating feeders and baths. The most common one would probably be bird baths and bird feeders, but there are other types that could be made to attract a wider variety of wildlife. Instead of putting birdfeed, you could put in nuts and grains for squirrels. You could make a beehive feeder to attract potential plant pollinators. With the types of plants and trees that you have in the garden, you can possibly attract or repel certain kinds of birds, bats, insects, and a variety of small rodents. This is not a bad thing, as they can help in fertilization, pollination, and spread of the plant species.

Arbors, Gazebos and Small Shelters

You can create rooms with a view with the use of vines, canopies, and pergolas as the "walls" and "roof" of your outdoor room. Hide from the harsh glare of the sun with little shelters that provide well needed shade during the warm months of the year. With a stable structure to grow on, plants can be used to create seemingly living walls that offer enough coverage for privacy and seclusion. You can create little spaces with intimate seating that is an ideal setting for romantic dinners and dates. Roses can be grown on an arbor to form a natural roof that is all at once functional, beautiful, and sweet smelling.

Mazes and Other Curiosities

Hedge mazes have been traditional features in medieval garden. You can relive those times by creating a maze of your own by using hedges as well or more modern and progressive materials. The choice is up to you, depending on the overall theme of your garden. Another interesting idea would be to create a winding path or a long flight of steps that leads to a grotto or shrine. Aside from adding interest, it feeds the spiritual quality of the outdoor living space. You could put in manmade caves or maybe a wishing well as points of interest. If you are fortunate enough to have natural water forms within your property such as streams or a lake, enjoy them and take advantage of their natural beauty. Create waterfront structures like a small pier or landing where you could moor a boat. You can have bathing houses or changing rooms close to the area for more convenience.

Hiding Places, Hidden Treasure, and Mystery

Create an aura of mystery by putting in little hidden treasures that are surprisingly pleasant. You can place a small fountain behind a hedge for example, or put a miniature play house behind some tress at the very edge of your property. Guests will be especially delighted when they discover this treasure. You can hide secret gardens behind walls and fences for a little intrigue and to attract the viewer's curiosity.

Tunnels, Vines, and Trellises

You can create a green tunnel by training flexible plants to grow and form overhead. This not only gives and enchanting feel to the place but also provides needed shading from the sun when the opportunity arrives. You can use trellises to train vines to grow over the walls of your house, creating a sort of living carpet or wall paper. Flowering vines can add color if green is not a particular favorite. Vines can be made to grow to make canopies that function as outdoor roofing for shade and shelter.

A Quiet Place for Retreat

There are times when we all need a break from the stresses of the world. You can create an avenue of escape by placing little quiet nooks for peace and meditation right in your own garden or yard. You can put in benches, chairs, pillows, mats, rugs, or even a hammock or day bed to add comfort. Bamboo fountains, meditating stones, and crystals could be incorporated into the design for an extra calming effect. Screens and hedges can be strategically positioned for optimum privacy and seclusion. You can put an adjustable shade on the patio so you can use it during both dry and wet weather, while providing you with ample space to be alone. A Zen oasis can be created with a minimalist theme; the good thing about this is that it is simple to build and there are fewer plants to be maintained, in keeping with the clean lines concept.

Fairytales and Other Themes

The ultimate touch of whimsy is creating a fairytale book like environment, complete with possibly about to talk flowers, colorful butterflies, sparkling lights, and maybe a sparkling pond or tinkling mini waterfall. Creating themes for your garden can help you have a focus on the direction that you want to go. You could maybe create a one color per area garden by planting those that only have purple flowers, for example. You can recreate the desert right in your backyard with sand, cacti, and some gravel, boulders or stones. You can add in some ornamental figures to further strengthen the theme: statues of Roman goddesses and nymphs, frog statues for the pond, fairy lights for the trees, scarecrows, mystical crystal markers, ethnic masks and shields, native jars and bowls, bridges, miniature castles, mini Ferris wheels, slides, etc. There are a million and one ways to design your space. The only limits are your creativity and imagination.

Conclusion

An elegant garden does not just appear overnight. The best elegant gardens have been carefully planned. You don't have to be a landscape architect to plan the perfect escape either.

As you sit down to write your plan, consider the following:

Where does the sun fall on your garden and at what time?

Before you start making a blueprint of where everything goes, you need to note where and when the sunlight falls on your yard. This is important if you want to incorporate a nice dining area which will be dappled in shade at the appropriate dining hours, or a sun bathing area next to your pool that is sheltered for children to play.

How much privacy do you already have and how much do you want?

If you have nosy neighbors and an open yard, or your home rests at the bottom of a hill, then you may need to incorporate tall trees or a trellis so that you can block the view that your neighbors get.

Do you need an outside tap?

If your yard does not already have a tap which you can use to connect to a hose, then you may need to have one installed before you can properly irrigate your yard. This can be useful for those with children who will need to fill up a small wading pool in the summer or set up a sprinkler to sit in the middle of the lawn.

Then you have to work out any practical matters.

Does your design need to cater to a family? Does it need to cater to family pets? Is its purpose to host social events? Will the design cater to just you and your spouse?

Remember to consider the needs of everyone who will be enjoying the elegant garden escape. If you have a dog that likes to play in your flowerbeds then it may be best to reconsider delicate flowers that will only be trampled. If you have children, you need to consider the safety of your design. A water feature without a basin may be better suited than a pond for families with small children.

Lastly, you must consider any storage you may

need. If you have garden furniture that is not weather proof, then you may need to make room for a shed that can store the furniture, bikes, toys for your pool, etc...

The design of your elegant garden should be made to fit your space, large or small. If, for instance, you have a view then you will want to craft a relaxing space that opens up toward the view. If you instead are surrounded by nosy neighbors, you may want to create a sense of privacy around a central area. Creating the perfect elegant garden is a combination of plants and ambience. Ambience is the result of the whole project. This means the manner in which the plants flows together, the shape of the garden, the lighting, any water features, furniture, and accessories. You can mix and match colors and styles to create unique ambiences all their own. You can mix and match materials such as concrete, rocks, stone, or wood.

There are many materials that you can use in your elegant garden. Composite bender boards are the best for footpaths and walkways as well because it doesn't rot and it bends easily. Wood would rot and does not bend as much. It must be replaced often. Concrete can be decorative but it isn't very elegant. Stones and pavers are also nice.

Consider the type of growing environment that your garden/yard offers. If there is a particular plant you absolutely must have in your yard, then you will have to research the best spot for it. If you want to incorporate flowering plants, vegetables, and/or fruit, you must find areas that get at least six hours of sun each day. If you have any area that is lightly shaded, or you can build one, then you have many more choices open to you. If you live in an area that is particularly windy, then you might want to clear the site of all garden weeds each week because the wind will cause your plants to shed rubbish habitually. It is recommended that you clear out the dead leaves and other weeds each week for windy areas.

You then have to check your soil. You can conduct home tests to analyze the quality of your soil with DIY soil test kits. You can get these from any garden center. They help you to measure the pH in your soil. If your readings indicate pH above 7 then your soil has high alkalinity, whereas a reading below 7 is acidic. Almost all soil ranges between 5.0 and 7.50. If yours does not, that is ok. You can find plants that fit highly alkaline soils or acidic soil.

Just a note: if you are buying your plants from a garden center or green house, you should check their labels for information on the pH preference. If there is none listed, the plants will do fine in neutral soil.

In addition to the pH of your soil, you should check the texture. Some soil is very heavy with clay, while other soil is sandy or rocky. The ideal texture is a sandy loam but if yours is not like this, it can be fixed with organic matter like compost.

CPSIA information can be obtained
at www.ICGtesting.com
Printed in the USA
BVHW081528070521
606759BV00010B/1859